ACROSS THE JEWNIVERSE

180 TOTALLY RANDOM JEWISH FACTS

Kerry Olitzky and
Deborah Bodin Cohen

To Dr. James Dowdell III and Zachary Levy, PA, healers of body, mind, and soul.
—K.O.

To the children of Congregation Beth Chai.
—D.B.C.

Apples & Honey Press, An Imprint of Behrman House Publishers, Millburn, New Jersey 07041, www.applesandhoneypress.com
ISBN 978-1-68115-687-3
Text copyright © 2025 by Kerry Olitzky and Deborah Bodin Cohen
Lexile® 910L
All rights reserved. No part of this publication may be translated, reproduced, stored in a retrieval system or transmitted, in any form or by any means, electronic, mechanical, photocopying, recording or otherwise, for any purpose, without express written permission from the publishers.

Library of Congress Cataloging-in-Publication Data
Names: Olitzky, Kerry M., author. | Cohen, Deborah Bodin, 1968- author.
Title: Across the Jewniverse : 180 random Jewish facts / by Kerry Olitzky and Deborah Bodin Cohen.
Description: Millburn, New Jersey : Apples & Honey Press, [2025] | Includes bibliographical references and index. | Audience: Ages 8-12 | Audience: Grades 4-6 | Summary: "180 surprising and fun facts about the Jewish people and culture drawn from a mere 5,000 years of history"-- Provided by publisher.
Identifiers: LCCN 2024061778 | ISBN 9781681156873 (paperback)
Subjects: LCSH: Jews--Juvenile literature.
Classification: LCC DS118 .O24 2025 | DDC 909/.04924--dc23/eng/20250220
LC record available at https://lccn.loc.gov/2024061778

Image Sources — Freepik: Front Cover TL, 3L, 63L (menorah) atlascompany, 6 (bkgd) kjpargerer, 7, 144 (Mr. Potato Head) rabiikhan5616, 7B xadartstudio, 8T mrmake, 9R (pants) tohamina, 9R (pepper) rawpixel, 10 (bkgd) tawatchai07, 10L freepik, 11L 3DSculptor, 11R, Back Cover (dreidel) pixel-shot, 12-13 (bkgd) freepik, 57 (bkgd) topntp26, 57B (brick) lifeforstock, 60 (bkgd) tawatchai07, 71B, Back Cover (tiara) gazisabbirmahmud420, 77 wayhomestudio, 78L jiffyavril, 81T Muhammad.abdullah, 91B freepik, 99 user2683494, 104T vecstock, 106L waverbreak media, 106-107 (car) handmadefont, 107C fotobomb,130 (bkgd) freepik, 130B freepik, 131 bunnyhop, 133TL (person) freepik, 134L shustrik, 134-135C arissu, 135 (bkgd) rawpixel, 136 (bkgd) romansigaev, 137 (cowboy) fazriyabegum82, 138-139 freepik, 140L (hummus) denira21, 140C (apple) freepik, 140R (oil) freepik, 140 (bkgd) freepik, 141T micro_studio, 141B elenakabenkina, 142-143 kstudio, 144 (books) wahyu_t. Envato Elements: Cover (bkgd) wirestock, Front Cover TR photobalance, Front Cover TC mrdoomits, Back Cover, 3TL (matzah) photovs, Front Cover BR, 35B spencerpa440, 3R mmoskalu, 3 (bkgd) LightFieldStudios, 3TR kelseno6, 8-9 (bkgd) didesign, 13 (Masada) foodphotoalex, 13, 37, 127L (polaroid frame) AntonioGravante, 14L Mint_Images, 16 (bkgd) edb3_16, 16 (flock) wirestock, 17 Lifeonwhite, 18T GoDoodle, 19bkgd wirestock, 19 (cactus) AtlasComposer, 20L Edalin, 25 (bkgd) M-e-f, 28-29 (bkgd) phichatp, 29B Nadianb, 30 traimakivan, 31T (brick) dezign56, 32 nuwatphoto, 33 Lifeonwhite / Edited by Alex Segal, 34 WildMediaSK, 35T vinnikava, 36L Lifeonwhite, 36 (bkgd) wirestock, 36R vvoennyy, 37TR picturepartners, 38TR natika, 38-39B pioneer111, 38-39 (bkgd) Mint_Images, 39R bowonpats, 40 edb3_16, 41T YuriArcursPeopleimages, 41B Rimidolove, 42 Sunny_studio, 43 Lifeonwhite, 44 Simol1407, 45 WMrapids, 46 zhenny-zhenny, 47T ABBPhoto, 50-51 (bkgd) maxxyustas, 51T mrdoomits, 52-53 wirestock, 56T antonpetrus, 57B (shoes) tenkende, 58 LightFieldStudios, 61 SeanPavone, 63R Lifeonwhite, 64-65 (bkgd) halfpoint, 66-67 (bkgd) miraclemoments, 66-67 (medal) BrianAJackson, 68 (bkgd) chones, 68 ozaiachin, 69, Back Cover TL (bats) ozaiachin, 70 stockfilmstudio, 72 rthanuthattaphong, 73 (bkgd) Coastaltype, 74 seventyfourimages, 75 NomadSoul1, 76 LightFieldStudios, 78-79 Deniskarpenkov, 80 joaquincorbalan, 81B haveseen, 82L travellersnep, 82R fokkebok, 83T seventyfourimages, 83B, Back Cover TR orcearo, 88 (bkgd) kenishirotie, 88B creativetacos, 89 (bkgd) LightFieldStudios, 90L LightFieldStudios, 90-91 (bkgd) alisachikov, 91R (food) mmoskalyuk160462, 93R Ha4ipuri, 95 (bkgd) Lightboxx, 96-97 (notebook) natika, 104B Lifeonwhite, 108 (clay faces) dasha11, 108 (vaccine) wirestock, 110L ikadapurhangus, 110B sea_wave, 111T stockimagefactory, 112 (bike) kathkarnowski, 112 (bkgd) hiv360, 113 (dog) Lifeonwhite, 114 Rawpixel, 116 (bkgd) Unai82, 116R Kufotos, 117TL gresei, 117R (ice cream) Ha4ipuri, 117B svitlanaozirna, 118B wirestock, 118T tatiana_bralnina, 119 (bkgd) StiahailoAnastasiia, 119L Icons8, 123 (baby) wirestock, 124 (bkgd) NomadSoul1, 124 (flag) FabrikaPhoto, 125 (right frame) vvoennyy, 126 chormail, 128-129 akophotography, 133BR wirestock, 136-137 (gold nuggets) kostiuchenko, 137B (locket) fruitcocktail. Wikimedia: 3C, 100T (bear) Smithsonian Museum of Natural History, 20B Jonathunder, 21T Orren Jack Turner, Princeton, N.J. / Modified by PM_Poon & later by Dantadd, 21B Willem van de Pol, 24 Karl Beutel, 25 Chicago Moffett, 26 Kadumago, 27 (bkgd) Reto Stöckl / NASA Goddard Space Flight Center, 27L CutOffTies, 31B Petty Officer 2nd Class Andrew Eder. Edits by Alexandra Segal, 37T (Peki-In) Fotocollectie Van de Poll, 50B Valerian Gribayedoff, 54-55B Linterna de Energizer, 54T Unknown author, 55B Jonathan Mauer, 59T Dosseman, 62 Zachi Evenor, 65 The Israel Kristal Family, 69BR US Military Photographer, 71T Vinayaraj, 84 Unknown author, 85 Pere Jean Domenge, 86T Unknown author, 87L MET DP834773, 92-93 israeltourism, 94 Origafoundation, 95L, 95R Los Angeles Daily News, 95C New York Police Department, 98 DPLA, 100B Evan-Amos, 101 Originally published by the Los Angeles Times. Photographer unknown; Restored by Adam Cuerden, 102L White House Staff Photographers Collection, 102-103B Pete Souza, 103 (paper) creativetacos,105 Google Art Project, 109T GlaxoSmithKline plc, 109B US ARMY MEDICAL DEPARTMENT CENTER AND SCHOOL, 111B Stuhrchacz, 120-121 Unknown author, 121T Pierre Gildesgame Maccabi Sports Museum, 123 (Ethiopic genesis) Author Unknown, 125 (right person) Foreign and Commonwealth Office, 127L MRC Laboratory of Molecular Biology, 127R Raymond Gosling – King's College London Archives, 132 Revital Salomon, 133T (stamps) Israel Philatelic Federation, 133B (bkgd) anonymous, 137B (Ray Frank) I.am.a.qwerty. Pixabay: 4-5 solihinkentjana, 15 Pearly Peach, 18B Jollymama, 22-23 eak_kkk, 47B lolorun, 60C ornaw. Smithsonian Institution: 31T, Back Cover L (phone) James Di Loreto & Brittany M. Hance. Pexels: 48 Sherman Trotz. Library of Congress: 55T Marion Post Wolcott

Continued on page 144

Design by Alexandra Segal, Edited by Dena Neusner, Printed in China

9 8 7 6 5 4 3 2 1

How big was the world's largest matzah ball?

Who wrote the poem on the Statue of Liberty?

Who created the first teddy bear?

Turn the pages to find out. . . .

Superman's birth name, **Kal-El,** comes from the Hebrew for "voice of God."

WHAT'S UP, DOC?

Voice actor Mel Blanc was the voice of Bugs Bunny, Daffy Duck, Tweety Bird, Porky Pig, and dozens of other cartoon characters.

After making dolls for his sisters from garden potatoes, inventor George Lerner invented **MR. POTATO HEAD.**

Many Romanian Jews use hollowed-out potatoes as their **MENORAHS.**

The Dead Sea is

ONE-THIRD SALT . . .

10 times saltier than the Atlantic and Pacific Oceans.

The Dead Sea is also the LOWEST SPOT ON EARTH.

Its surface is almost 1,500 feet — or a quarter mile — below sea level.

There's an old superstition among Russian Jews: Put salt in your pockets **TO KEEP DEMONS AWAY.**

Do you think a dreidel will spin in

OUTER SPACE?

Astronaut Jeffrey Hoffman might know. He packed one for his trip on the **SPACE SHUTTLE.**

By the way, a dreidel will **SPIN ENDLESSLY** in outer space, until it's interrupted.

Israeli scientists Dr. Elaine Solowey and Dr. Sarah Sallon grew palm trees from **2,000-YEAR-OLD SEEDS** found on Masada.

In the Italian village of Pitigliano (also known as Little Jerusalem), the old Jewish quarter is **UNDERGROUND,** with rooms carved into rock.

There are **"LITTLE JERUSALEM"** villages, towns, and neighborhoods in

* Burlington, Vermont
* Charleston, South Carolina
* Chelsea, Massachusetts
* Sarcelle, France

TWEET!

500 million birds migrate across Israel each year...

TWICE!

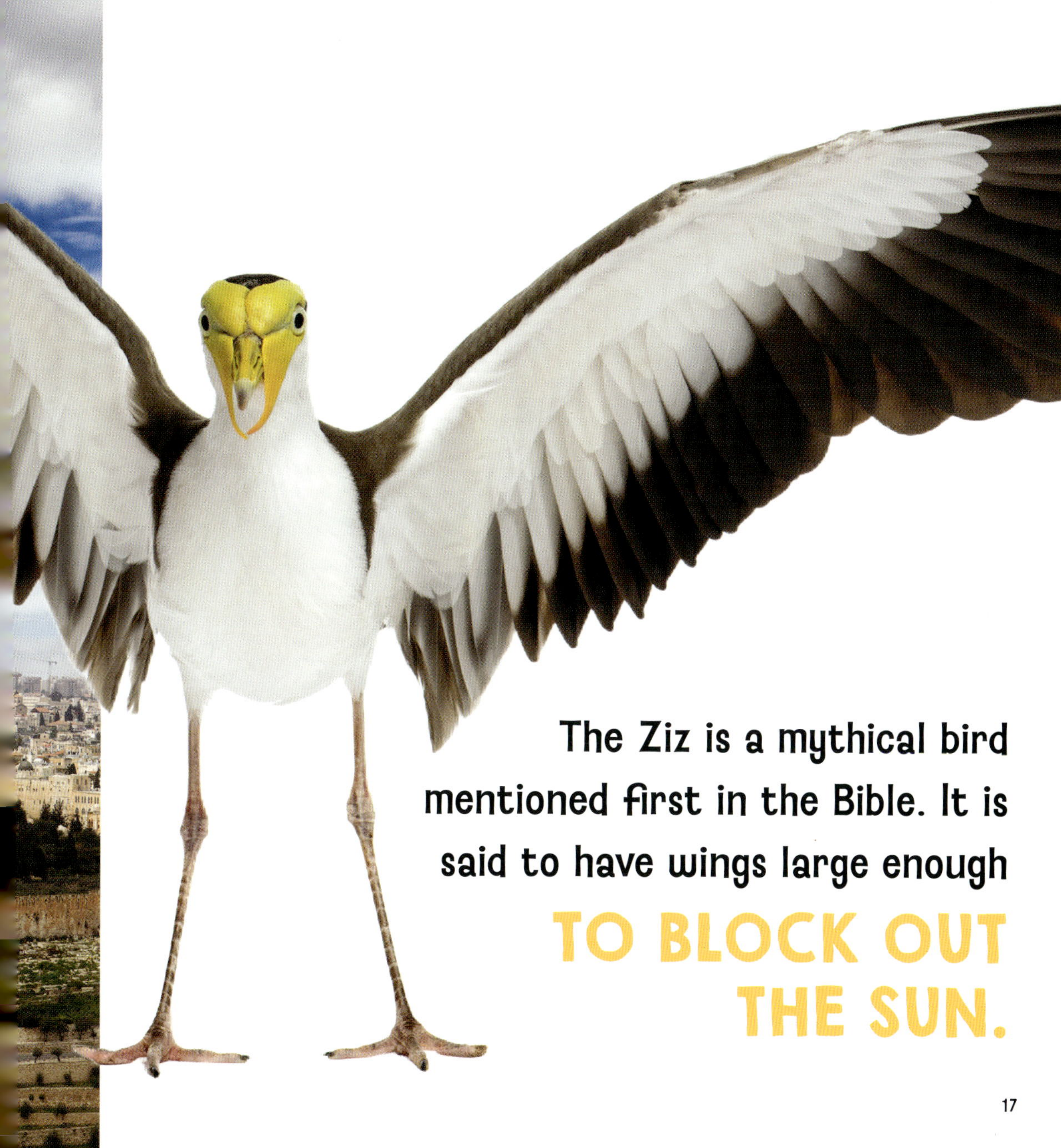

The Ziz is a mythical bird mentioned first in the Bible. It is said to have wings large enough **TO BLOCK OUT THE SUN.**

A native-born Israeli is called a **SABRA** in Hebrew, after a cactus fruit with a **THORNY,** tough skin and a **SWEET** interior.

from Mexico

to Israel

Ironically, cacti aren't native to Israel. Spanish explorers brought them from **MEXICO** to the Middle East about 500 years ago.

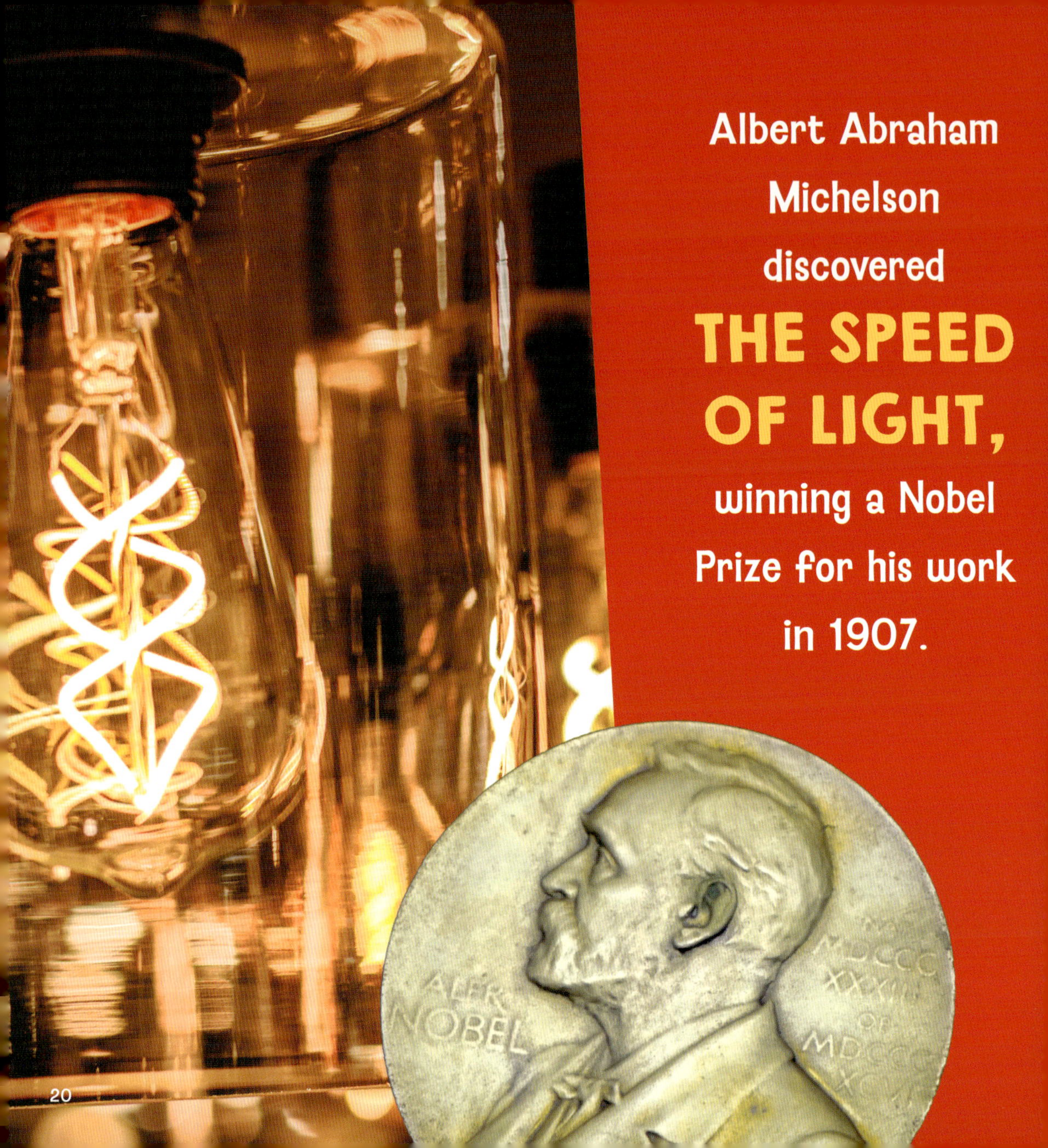

Albert Abraham Michelson discovered **THE SPEED OF LIGHT,** winning a Nobel Prize for his work in 1907.

Another Albert: Zionist leaders asked Albert Einstein to be Israel's **SECOND PRESIDENT.** (Einstein declined.)

Prime Minister Golda Meir was the first modern **FEMALE HEAD OF STATE** in the Middle East and only the fourth elected in the world.

SMALL BUT MIGHTY. TAKE A GUESS:

How many people in the **WORLD** are Jewish?

A. 1 out of every 5 people

B. 1 out of every 50 people

C. 1 out of every 500 people

How many Nobel Prize **WINNERS** are Jewish?

A. 1 out of every 4 winners

B. 1 out of every 40 winners

C. 1 out of every 400 winners

(Answers: Population—C; Nobel winners—A)

THE *TITANIC*, the largest ship of its time, served kosher food and offered Jewish prayer services. Several hundred Jews traveled on the *Titanic*. Only **27 SURVIVED** after the "unsinkable" ship sank in 1912.

Titanic survivor Irene Wallach Harris became **BROADWAY'S FIRST** female theater manager and producer.

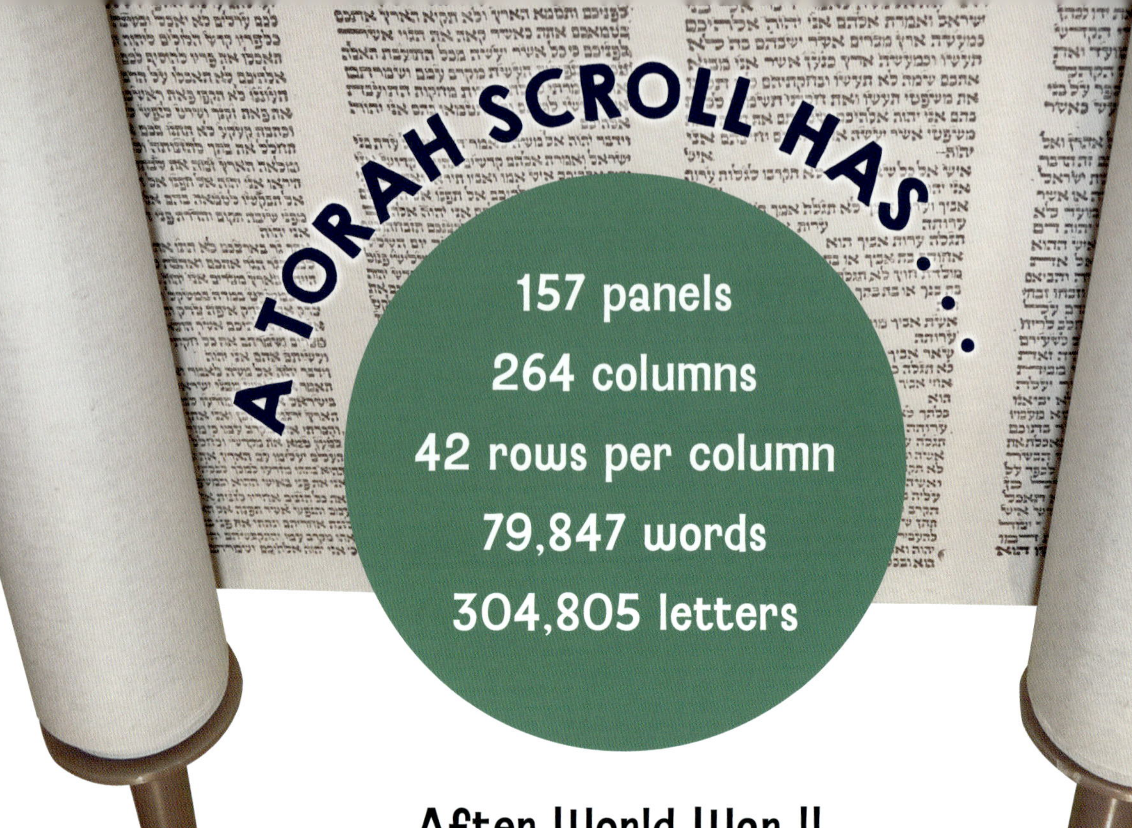

After World War II,

1,564 TORAH SCROLLS

from destroyed synagogues were brought to London. They're now on loan to synagogues worldwide from Chattanooga, Tennessee, to Tasmania, Australia.

Tasmania's Hobart Synagogue was built in 1845 on land donated by Judah Solomon, a

BRITISH EX-CONVICT

who had been shipped off to Australia as punishment for being a thief.

LE CHOCOLAT!

Jews fleeing the Spanish Inquisition built the first chocolate factories in

FRANCE.

In 1650, a Turkish Jewish trader known as Jacob the Jew opened England's first coffeehouse and served **HOT CHOCOLATE.**

AFTER
THE
BEEP . . .
Voicemail
technology
was developed
in Israel.

Martin Cooper unveiled the **FIRST CELL PHONE** in 1972. The phone was so large and clunky, it was nicknamed “the brick.”

ACTRESS OR INVENTOR?

Although Hedy Lamarr is best known as a movie star from the 1930s to 1950s, she also invented technology used in Wi-Fi, GPS, and Bluetooth communications.

"Hatikvah" wasn't declared Israel's official national anthem until 2004,

56 YEARS

after Israel's founding.

Many European folk songs share the "Hatikvah" melody, including a **SLOVENIAN CHILDREN'S SONG,** "The Little Owl Got Married."

Israel's national bird, the hoopoe, gives off a **VERY STINKY ODOR** in its nest to protect its chicks.

Talking about stinky animals . . . over 4,500 **CAMELS** live in Israel.

Camels can run **40 MILES PER HOUR** and drink 40 gallons of water at a time. Camels have two sets of **EYELASHES** and three sets of **EYELIDS** to keep out sand.

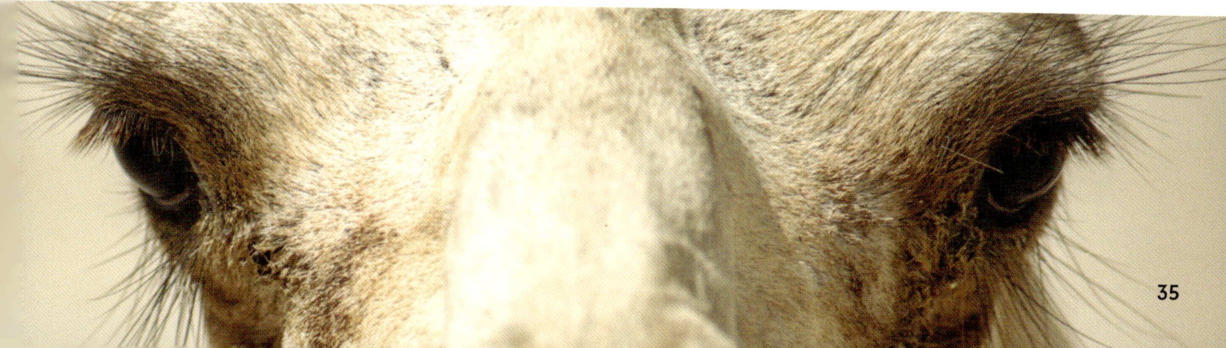

GOT YOUR SHOVEL? Jerusalem has over 2,000 active archaeological sites.

The largest stone in the Western Wall is 44 feet long and weighs 570 tons—as much as

100 ELEPHANTS.

The Old Synagogue in Peki'in, Israel, was built in the 3rd or 4th century CE using stones from the ruins of the Second Temple. Only **ONE KEY** to the synagogue exists, and it's passed down from generation to generation in a family that has lived in Peki'in since that time.

LICORICE BREAD? Many Jewish bakers of Moroccan descent shape their challahs like flowers and flavor them with anise, which tastes similar to licorice.

The world's biggest challah was 35 feet, 2 inches long—about the **LENGTH OF A SCHOOL BUS.**

Ugandan Jews bake challah in

BANANA LEAVES.

Jerusalem has been conquered

MORE THAN 40 TIMES.

The word *Jerusalem* means **"CITY OF PEACE"** in Hebrew.

Israel covers **LESS THAN ONE PERCENT** of the land in the Middle East.

An estimated 20 percent of

AMERICAN MAGICIANS

are Jewish.

ABRACADABRA

comes from the Hebrew for "I will create as I speak."

TA-DA!

The father of famous magician Harry Houdini was a rabbit. No, a rabbi!

Archaeologists in Israel have dug up evidence of 9,000-year-old **BOARD GAMES.**

Ralph Baer, a refugee from Nazi Germany, invented the world's **FIRST VIDEO GAME CONSOLE**. Its black-and-white screen was capable of displaying only one vertical line and three moving dots.

The land of Israel's record

HIGH TEMPERATURE

is 129 degrees fahrenheit, set in 1942.

In 1950, Israel had 3 feet, 4 inches

OF SNOW.

Eilat, at the southern tip of Israel, gets only

ONE INCH OF RAIN

each year. Some perspective: Miami gets 60 inches of rain annually.

JEWS AS SUPERHEROES:

Gal Gadot:
Wonder Woman

Andrew
Garfield:
Spider-Man

Scarlett
Johannson:
Black Widow

Aaron Taylor-
Johnson:
Quicksilver

Natalie
Portman:
Jane Foster

Gwyneth Paltrow:
Pepper Potts

Paul Rudd:
Ant-Man

Fredericka Mandelbaum was the first **ORGANIZED CRIME BOSS** in New York City. She masterminded numerous bank robberies and heists of luxury goods.

Eastern State Penitentiary in Philadelphia housed so many Jewish convicts that they built the **FIRST PRISON SYNAGOGUE** in 1924.

WRITE ON!

Individuals place more than 1 million personal prayers in the Western Wall each year.

Dear God,
I'm writing today to ask you for help with my

Twice a year, before Rosh Hashanah and Passover, the notes are collected and
BURIED.
The Israeli Postal Company has a
"LETTERS TO GOD"
department.
Answers are not guaranteed.

In 1931,
Lásló Bíró invented
the ballpoint pen.

WHO INVENTED THAT?

The world's first flashlight was built in the 1890s by Conrad Hubert (born Akiba Horowitz).

Supermarket owner Sylvan Nathan Goldman invented the **SHOPPING CART** in 1936.

CLICK!

Edwin Land invented the Polaroid, the first instant camera, in 1947.

85 percent of Israelis use

SOLAR POWER–

more than any other country on earth.

HEY, DUDE!

Most Israelis have a "dude shemesh," otherwise known as a solar water heater, on their roof.

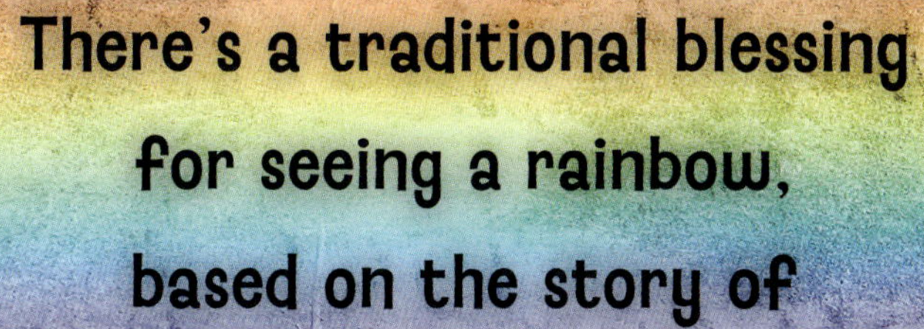

There's a traditional blessing for seeing a rainbow, based on the story of **NOAH AND THE ARK.**

Yip Harburg and Harold Arlen wrote the lyrics and composed the music to **"OVER THE RAINBOW,"** featured in *The Wizard of Oz*.

Pass the jelly donuts!

Israelis consume

24 MILLION *SUFGANIYOT*

during Hanukkah.

The menorah was the original Jewish symbol, not the Star of David.

The world's **LARGEST MENORAH** stands 32 feet tall and weighs 4,000 pounds. Find it every Hanukkah near New York's Central Park.

Jews in Alaska call themselves the "FROZEN CHOSEN."

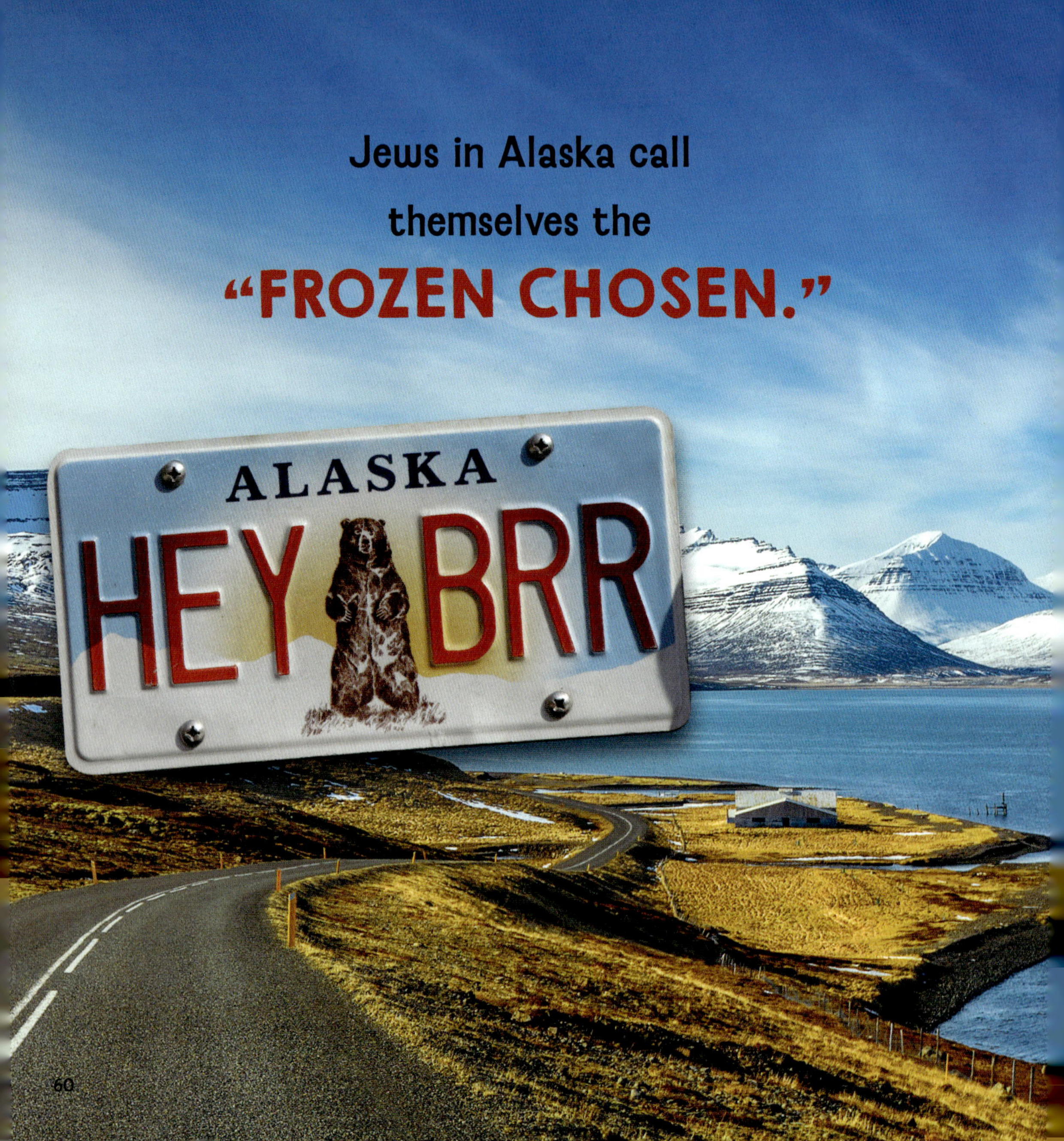

Jews in Denver, which has an elevation of one mile above sea level, say they live a

“MILE CHAI.”

The Pilgrims modeled the first Thanksgiving after **SUKKOT.**

THANKSGIVUKKAH (NOUN):

When Thanksgiving and Hanukkah overlap.

Last occurrence: 2013

Next occurrence: 2070

In 1922, 12-year-old Judith Kaplan celebrated her

BAT MITZVAH.

She was the first girl to observe that rite of passage. She noted (years later), that “No thunder sounded. No lightning struck.”

In 2016, Yisrael Kristal celebrated his bar mitzvah at the **AGE OF 113**. He had missed out on a bar mitzvah 100 years earlier due to World War I. Guests included his 2 children and many of his 9 grandchildren and 32 great-grandchildren.

SPLASH! Swimmer Mark Spitz set 33 world records and won 11 Olympic medals.

Only swimmer
Dara Torres, with
12 MEDALS,
beat Spitz as the
most successful
Jewish Olympian.

Playing from 1866 to 1881,
left-handed slugger
Lipman Pike was MLB's
FIRST HOME RUN
CHAMPION.

What are the chances? On a single day, June 8, 2018, five different Jewish MLB players **ALL HIT HOME RUNS.**

THE HEBREW HAMMER! Five-time All-Star Hank Greenberg played for Detroit from 1930 to 1946. His career was interrupted for several years when he joined the armed forces during World War II.

Jews have

LIVED IN INDIA

for nearly 2,600 years.

A neighborhood in Kochi, India, is called **JEW TOWN.**

Four Jewish women have been **CROWNED MISS INDIA.**

According to the Orthodox Union, 80 to 90 percent of New York City's kosher restaurants serve **SUSHI.**

There are 20 communal farms called kibbutzim

. . . IN JAPAN.

In the 1960s and 1970s, Japanese students went to Israel to learn the kibbutz way of life and bring it back to Japan.

54 percent of
CHESS CHAMPIONS
are Jewish.

Israeli Alik Gershom played chess with

523 OPPONENTS AT ONCE

— a world record.

He won 86 percent of the games.

Wilhelm Steinitz, the first world chess champion, was **UNBEATEN** for 32 years.

ACHOO!

Lithuanian Jews pull on their ears when sneezing.

Some Jews believe that if a person **SNEEZES WHILE TALKING,** whatever they were saying will happen.

No one knows how to pronounce **GOD'S NAME** in Hebrew.

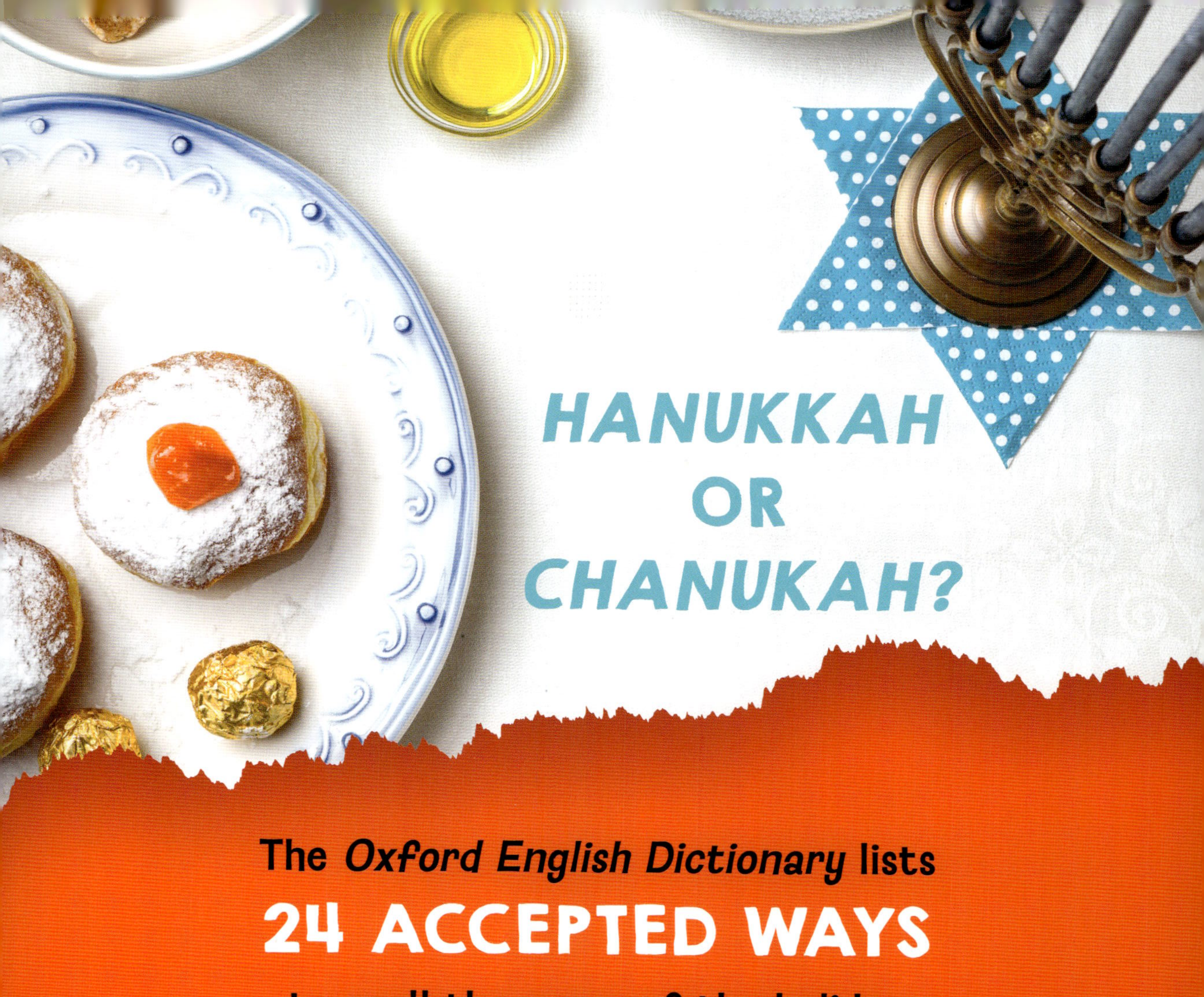

HANUKKAH OR CHANUKAH?

The *Oxford English Dictionary* lists **24 ACCEPTED WAYS** to spell the name of the holiday.

GIUDAICO-ROMANESCO

is the Jewish language spoken in Rome. Only about 250 people still speak it.

A delicacy from Rome—

PIZZA EBRAICA

or "Hebrew Pizza." Toppings: almonds, raisins, white wine, and olive oil.

Jews have lived in **ROME** for 2,200 years—longer than in any other European city.

Want to attend the world's largest Passover seder? Head to either

KATHMANDU, NEPAL,

or **PHUKAT, THAILAND.**

Both have seder meals with 2,000 or more guests.

To prepare for Passover, some Ethiopian Jews **THROW THEIR OLD PLATES TO THE GROUND** and make new ones to symbolize breaking from the past and getting a fresh start.

The clock's ticking! Matzah must be mixed and baked within **18 MINUTES** to be kosher for Passover.

The

CANTONESE

symbols for the name Abraham are

阿無羅漢

These symbols were engraved

500 YEARS AGO

on a stone in Kaifeng, China.

All of Kaifeng's Jews had one of

SEVEN LAST NAMES:

Ai, Gao, Jin, Li, Shi, Zhang, or Zhao.

The Jewish community in China dates back to the Northern Song Dynasty

北宋

(960-1127 CE).

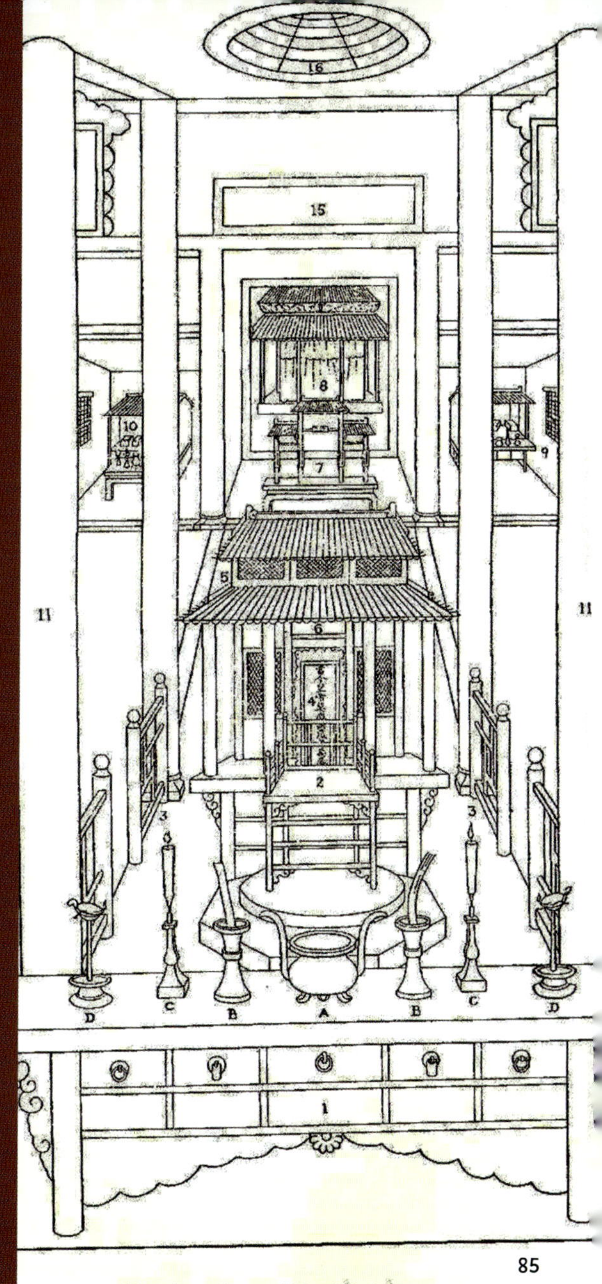

Interior view of the K'ai-fêng synagogue

BOO, HISS!
Judah Benjamin was the first Jewish attorney general and secretary of state in American history.
WAS HE A HERO? NOPE.
He supported slavery and served these roles for the Confederacy.

In 1862, future US president Ulysses S. Grant

EXPELLED ALL JEWS

from parts of Tennessee, Kentucky, and Mississippi.

Grant's Order #11 held for

ONE MONTH,

until Abraham Lincoln convinced Grant to repeal it.

General Grant's Order Expelling the Jews from Paducah, Ky.

GENERAL ORDER—NO. 11.

HEADQUARTERS THIRTEENTH ARMY CORPS, DEPARTMENT OF THE TENNESSEE, OXFORD, Miss., Dec. 17, 1862.

The Jews, as a class, violating every regulation of trade established by the Treasury Department, also department orders, are hereby expelled from the department within twenty-four hours from the receipt of this order by post commanders. They will see that all this class of people are furnished with passes and required to leave, and any one returning after such notification will be arrested and held in confinement until an opportunity occurs of sending them out as prisoners, unless furnished with permits from these headquarters. No passes will be given these people to visit headquarters for the purpose of making personal application for trade permits. By order of

Major General GRANT.

Jews made up nearly two-thirds of the white **FREEDOM RIDERS**—civil rights activists who rode buses to the South in the 1960s to protest segregation.

Carol Ruth Silver spent 40 days **IN JAIL** for attempting to use a waiting room marked "colored" in a bus station in Jackson, Mississippi.

In the Polish town Góra Kalwaria, seder goers **POUR WATER ON THE FLOOR** to remember the crossing of the Red Sea by the Israelites.

Jews of Gibraltar put

BRICK DUST

in their *charoset*.

A caveat: don't

try this at home.

An old Spanish custom:

the seder leader taps

the seder plate

THREE TIMES

on each guest's

HEAD

as a sign of blessing.

SURF'S UP!

Israel has 137 beaches.

SABABA סַבָּבָּה

means "cool," "great," or "awesome" in Hebrew slang, based on Arabic.

The world's northernmost coral reef is located in Eilat, Israel. After years of shrinking in size, the reef is **GROWING AGAIN,** thanks to Israeli environmental efforts.

Google Larry Page and Sergey Brin.

You'll learn that

THE PAIR CREATED

the Google search engine.

Do another online search, this time for

JEWISH GANGSTERS.

You'll undoubtedly learn the names

Bugsy Siegel, Meyer Lansky, and Mickey Cohen.

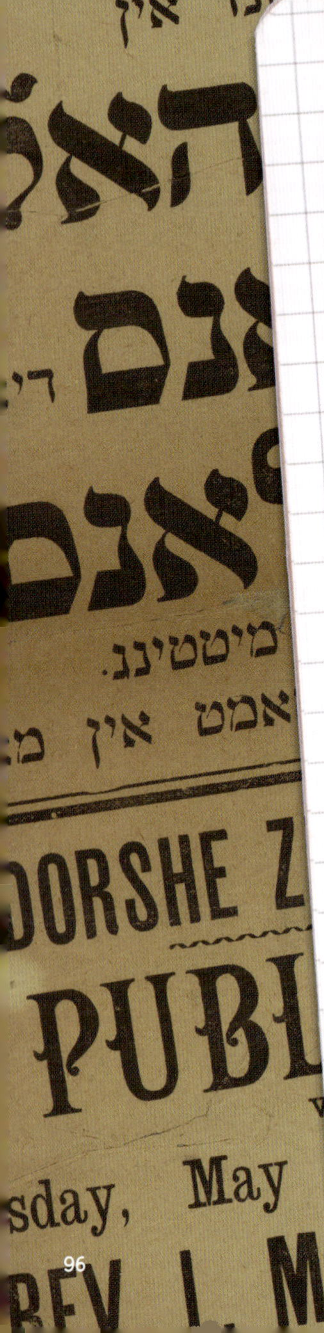

In Yiddish, the word

YIDDISH

means "Jewish."

In 1939,

11 MILLION PEOPLE

spoke Yiddish as their daily language. Today, fewer than 1 million do.

YIDDISH LESSON:

Klutz: A clumsy person

Kvetch: Complain

Mensch: A good, kind person

Meshugas: Craziness

Nosh: Snack

POW! In the 1920s and 1930s, one-third of all professional boxers were Jewish.

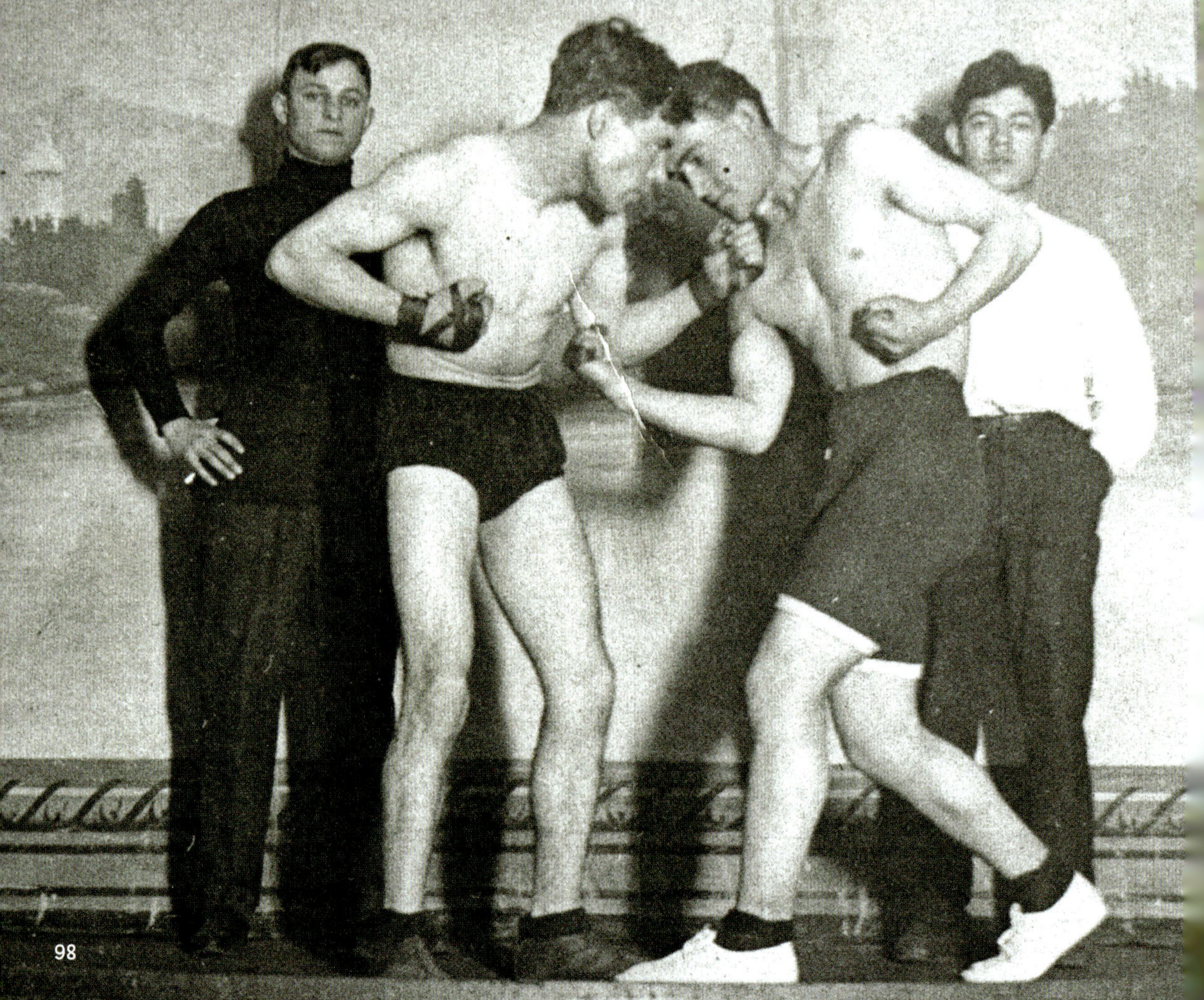

JEWISH WOMEN

also climbed into the boxing ring,
ncluding Carolina Raquel "La Turca" Duer of Argentina,
Hagar Finer of Israel,
and Sarah Deming of the United States.

In 1902, Jewish candy store owners Rose and Morris Michtom created the first

TEDDY BEAR–

in honor of President Theodore Roosevelt.

Leo Hirshfield created the Tootsie Roll in 1907, naming it after his daughter, who was

NICKNAMED TOOTSIE.

Ruth Handler created the **BARBIE DOLL** in 1959, naming it after her daughter, Barbara. (Yes, she also had a son named Ken.)

In 1979, Jimmy Carter was the **FIRST PRESIDENT** to light a menorah at the White House.

Clothing salesman Eddie Jacobson and President Harry Truman were best friends. Eddie often sent

CARE PACKAGES

to the White House filled with shirts, socks, and even underwear.

President Barack Obama hosted the first

WHITE HOUSE SEDER in 2009.

The

WORLD'S LARGEST MATZAH BALL

—created in Tucson, Arizona, in 2010—weighed 488 pounds! That's as big as an adult black bear.

In the 1500s, there were approximately 25 printed versions of the Haggadah. By the 1700s, there were 230 versions.

Today, it is estimated that there are well over **3,000 VERSIONS** of the Haggadah in print.

WHICH ISN'T AN ISRAELI INVENTION?

Mobileye: life-saving AI to prevent ca accidents

SniffPhone: it smells disease

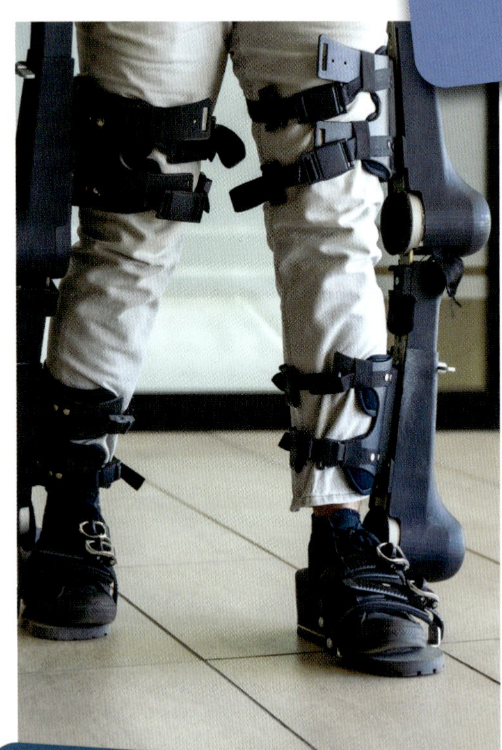

ReWalk: a battery-powered exoskeleton

Watergen: water produced from thin air

PillCam: a swallowable camera

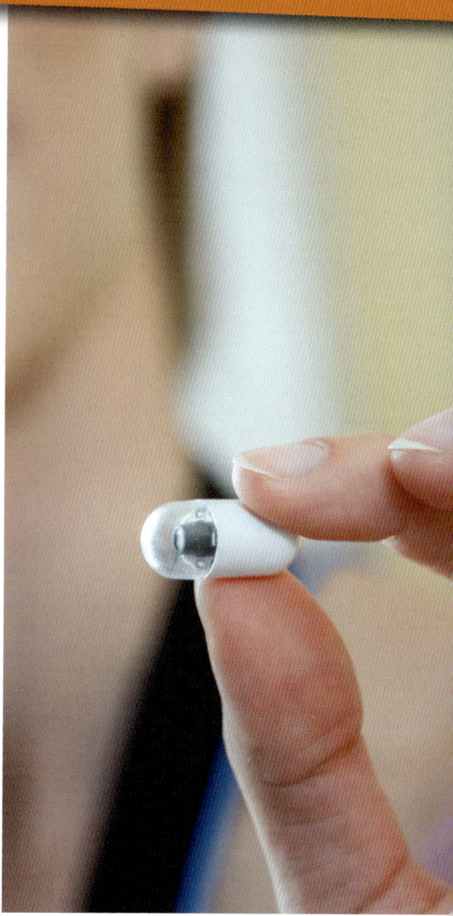

Trick question! They all were invented in Israel.

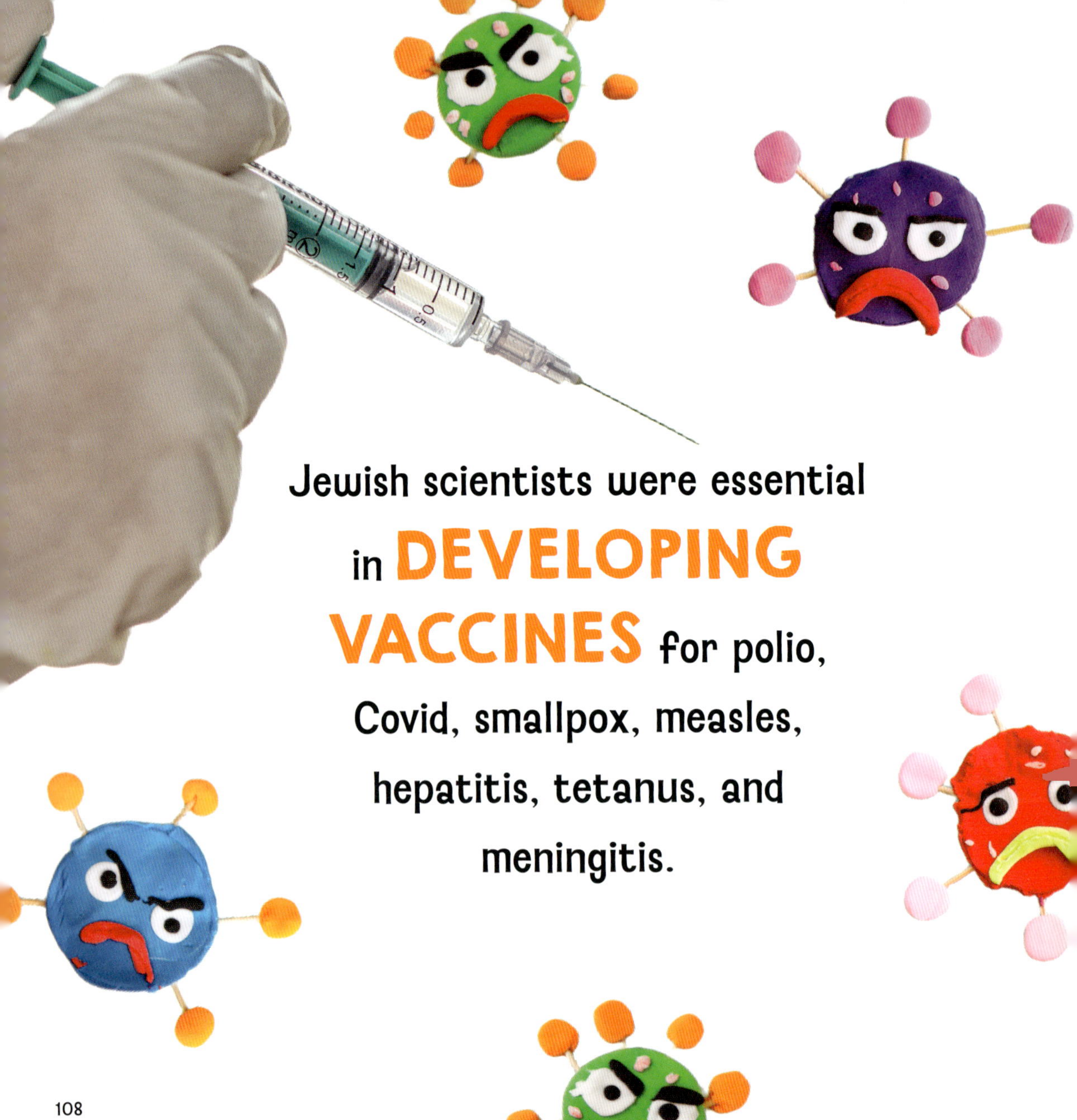

Jewish scientists were essential in **DEVELOPING VACCINES** for polio, Covid, smallpox, measles, hepatitis, tetanus, and meningitis.

Nobel winner Gertrude Elion **CREATED DRUGS TO FIGHT** leukemia, malaria, and autoimmune disorders.

Dr. Henry Heimlich discovered a maneuver to stop choking, aptly called, well, the **HEIMLICH MANEUVER.**

All around the world, Jewish chefs and bakers **FRY SPECIAL FOODS** for Hanukkah.

Italian Jews **FRY CHICKEN.**

Cuban and Puerto Rican Jews make latkes **OUT OF PLANTAINS.**

Egyptian Jews fry dough balls and dip them in **HONEY.**

Romanian Jews make filled donuts covered in **JAM AND SOUR CREAM.**

In 1894, Annie Londonderry became the first woman to

BIKE AROUND THE WORLD.

She wanted to raise awareness about women's rights and independence.

Helene Hines, who has multiple sclerosis, is a **CHAMPION HAND CYCLIST** and the first disabled person inducted into the National Jewish Sports Hall of Fame and Museum.

Morris Frank, who was blind, brought the first Seeing Eye dog to the United States, a German shepherd named **BUDDY.**

YIDDISH is known for great insults.
VAKSU Z
MITN KO
May your stomach rumble so badly, you'll think IT IS A GRAGGER (a Purim noisemaker).

TU VI A TSIBELE
N DR'ERD.

May you grow like an onion—**WITH YOUR HEAD IN THE GROUND.**

May all your teeth **FALL OUT** but one—and may that one get a toothache.

Found on an ancient Egyptian pottery shard, this recipe dates back to 1600 BCE, around the time the Israelites were slaves in Egypt:

ALMOND & DATE CANDY BALLS

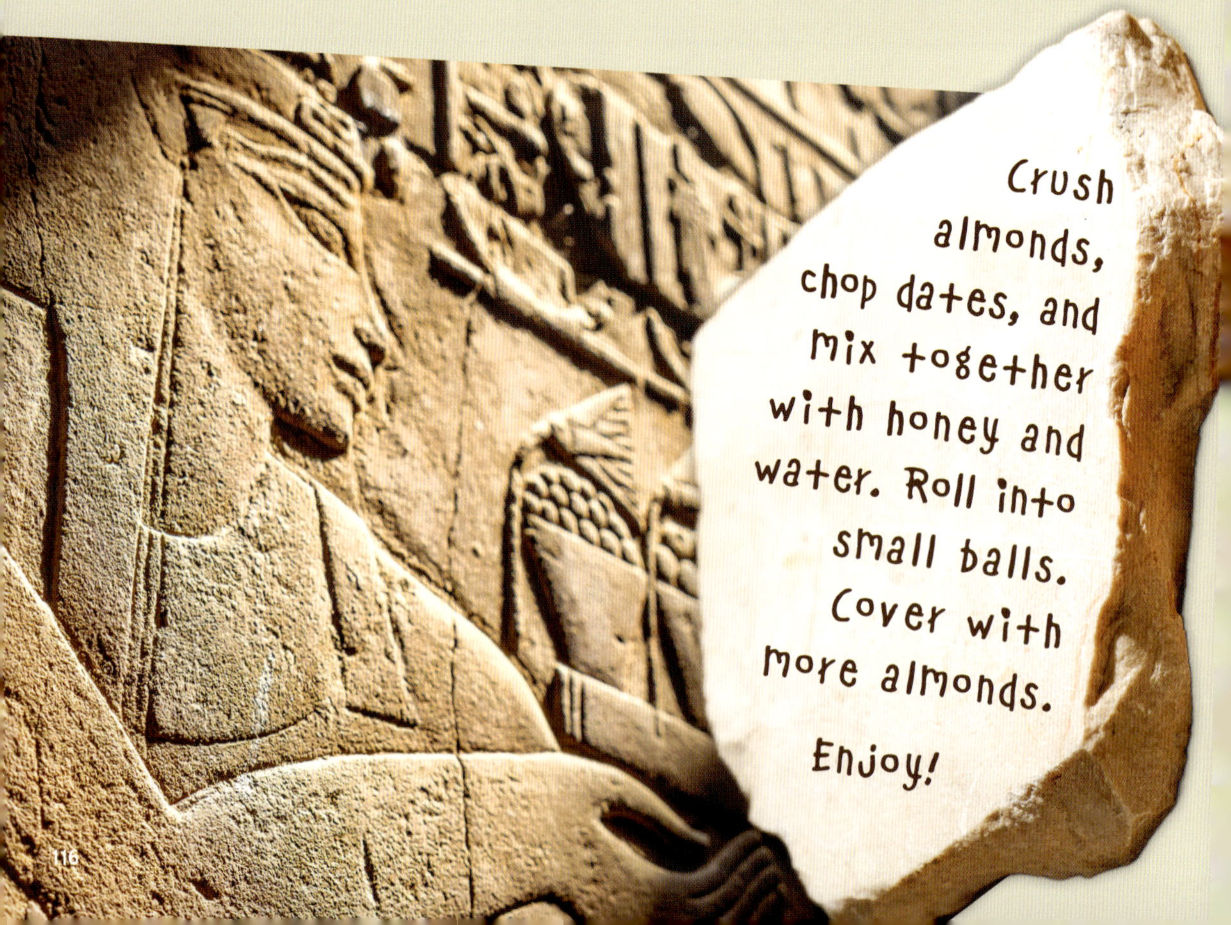

Do you like **LOLLIPOPS?**

SPRINKLES?

Chocolate-covered
ESKIMO PIES?

Thank Rabbi Sam Born.
In the early 1900s,
he invented the
technology to make
all three possible.

Daniel Herszberg has visited **EVERY COUNTRY** in the world—all before his 30th birthday. He sought out Jewish sites wherever he could.

102 countries have a Jewish population of **100 PEOPLE** or more.

Once, **40,000 JEWS** lived in Afghanistan. By 2005, only two Jews were left. The men hated each other and refused to speak to each other—even though they shared a home.

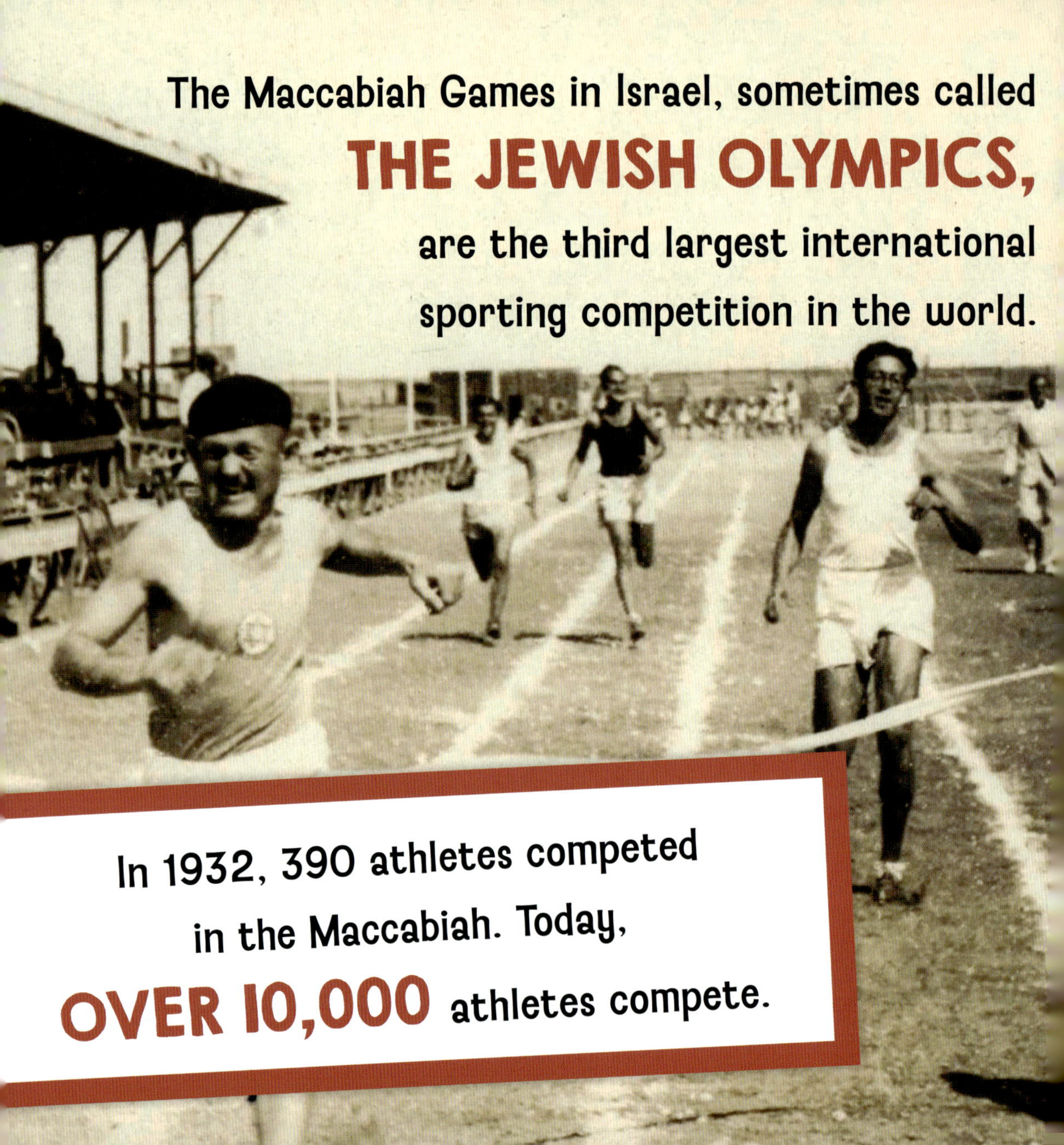

The Maccabiah Games in Israel, sometimes called **THE JEWISH OLYMPICS,** are the third largest international sporting competition in the world.

In 1932, 390 athletes competed in the Maccabiah. Today, **OVER 10,000** athletes compete.

In 1930 and 1931,

TWO MOTORCYCLE BRIGADES,

with 11 bikers each, drove over 9,000 miles to announce the first Maccabiah Games to the Jewish communities of Europe and North Africa.

Over 36 hours in May 1991, nonstop flights secretly brought **14,325** Ethiopian Jews to Israel.

The mission was called

OPERATION SOLOMON.

EIGHT BABIES

were born during the airlift.

In Ethiopia, Jews read their holy texts in the language **GE'EZ,** not Hebrew.

Why is this KNIGHT different from all OTHER KNIGHTS?

There have been **65 JEWISH KNIGHTS** in Great Britian.

The first Jewish knight was Sir Solomon de Medina, knighted in **1700.** In **2023,** King Charles knighted the chief rabbi of the United Kingdom, Ephraim Mirvis.

Genetic tests show that 40 percent of Ashkenazic Jews descend from just

FOUR WOMEN

of Middle Eastern origin who lived in Europe 1,000 years ago.

ROSALIND FRANKLIN

In the early 1950s, chemist Rosalind Franklin took the first **MICROSCOPIC PHOTO** of DNA.

About 3 MILLION eastern
European Jewish immigrants arrived
in the United States through
Ellis Island between
1880 and 1920.

Many settled on the Lower East Side in New York City, where it wasn't uncommon for a **FAMILY OF 10** to crowd into a 325-square-foot apartment. That's the size of an average hotel room.

The words "Give me your tired, your poor, your huddled masses . . ." on the Statue of Liberty were written by poet and activist **EMMA LAZARUS.**

Music legend Bob Dylan got his start playing guitar at **JEWISH SUMMER CAMP.** He went by Bobby Zimmerman back then.

Jewish composers wrote many of the most popular **CHRISTMAS CAROLS**—"White Christmas," "Rudolph, the Red-Nosed Reindeer," "Let It Snow! Let It Snow! Let It Snow!" and more.

Pocket change:

2,000-YEAR-OLD

coins, decorated with the image of the Temple menorah, have been found in Israel.

The name of the Israeli currency, the **SHEKEL,** dates back nearly 5,000 years to Akkadian, the most important language of the ancient Near East.

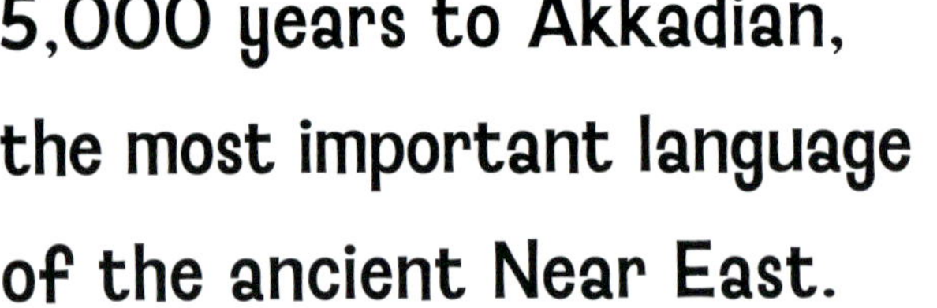

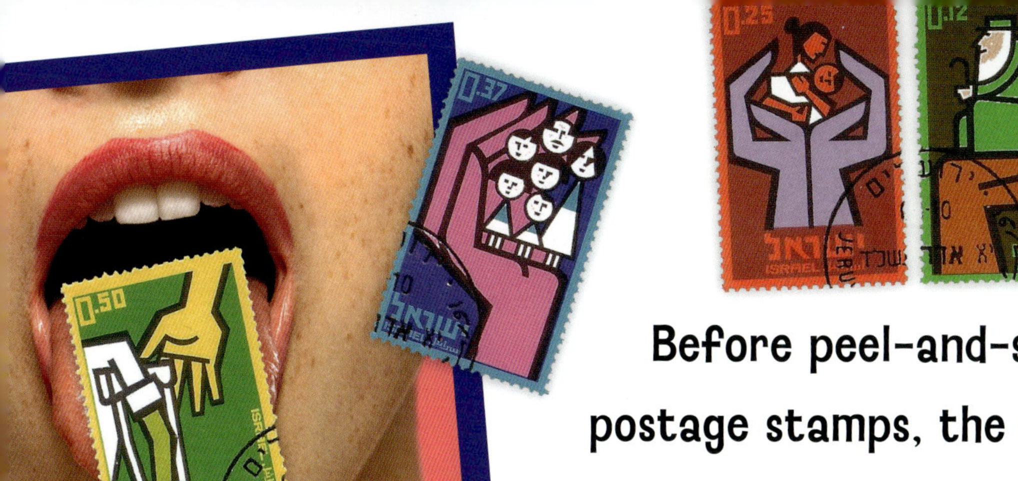

Before peel-and-stick postage stamps, the glue on the back of Israeli postage stamps was **KOSHER.**

Israeli money has **BRAILLE** on it.

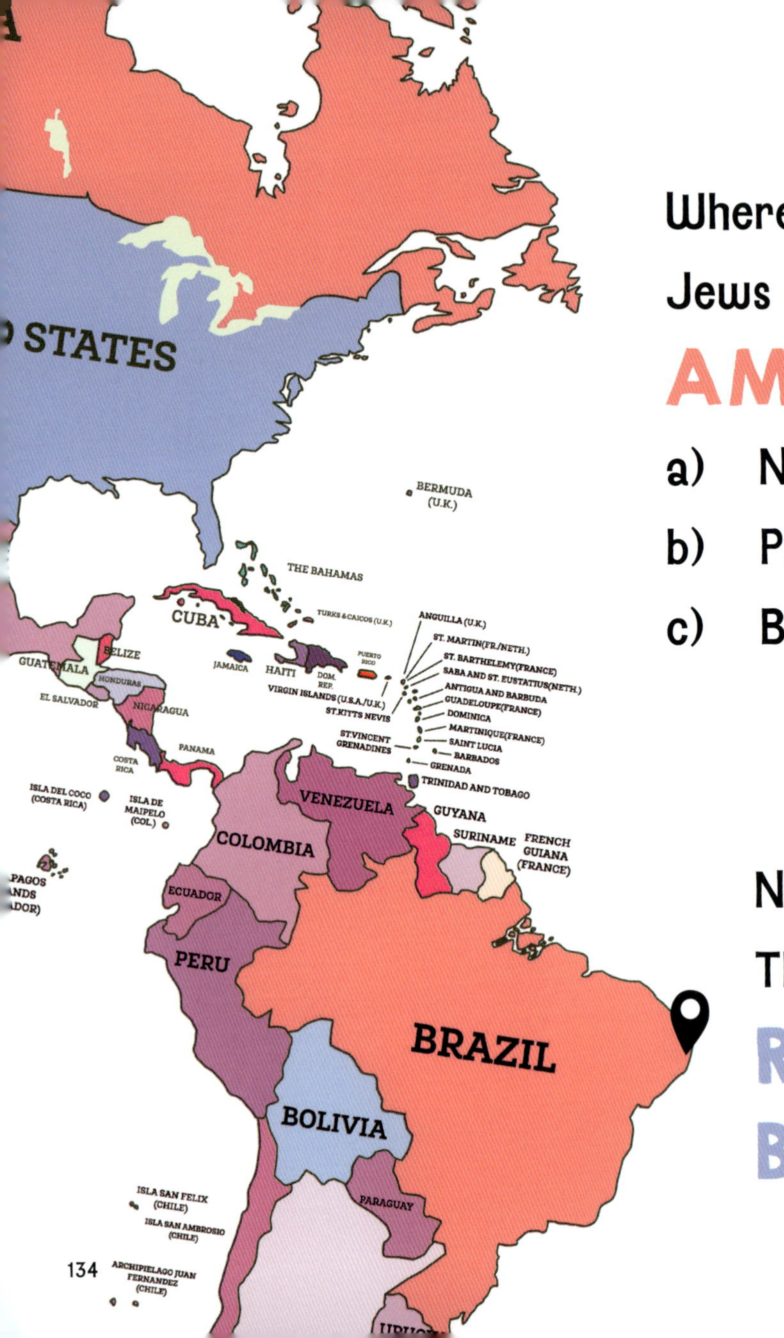

Where did the first Jews settle in the

AMERICAS?

a) New York?

b) Philadelphia?

c) Boston?

None of the above! They settled in

RECIFE, BRAZIL.

Luis de Torres, born Yosef ben HaLevi HaIvri, was the first Jewish person to set foot in the Americas. He traveled with

CHRISTOPHER COLUMBUS

as an interpreter.

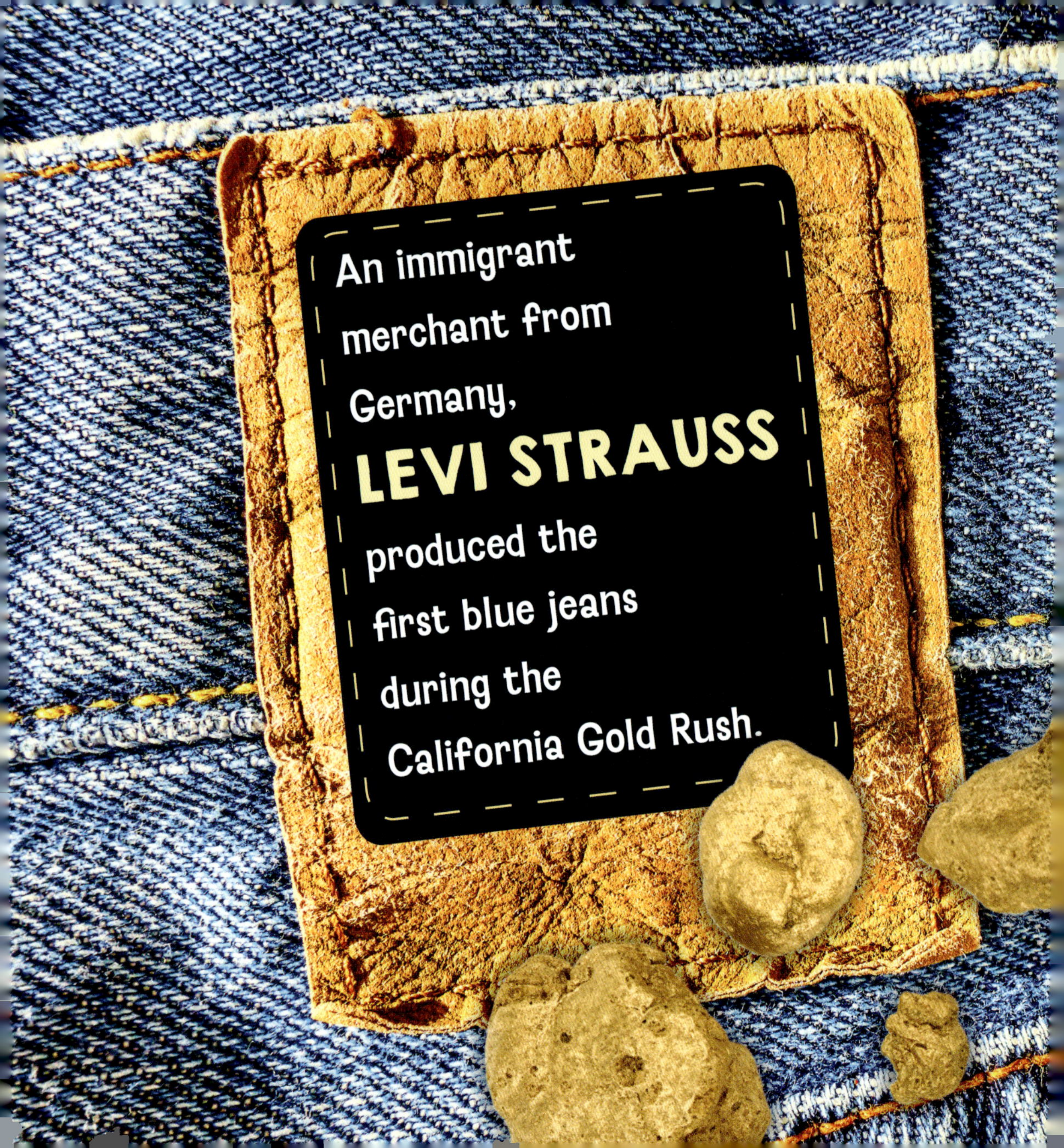
An immigrant
merchant from
Germany,
LEVI STRAUSS
produced the
first blue jeans
during the
California Gold Rush.

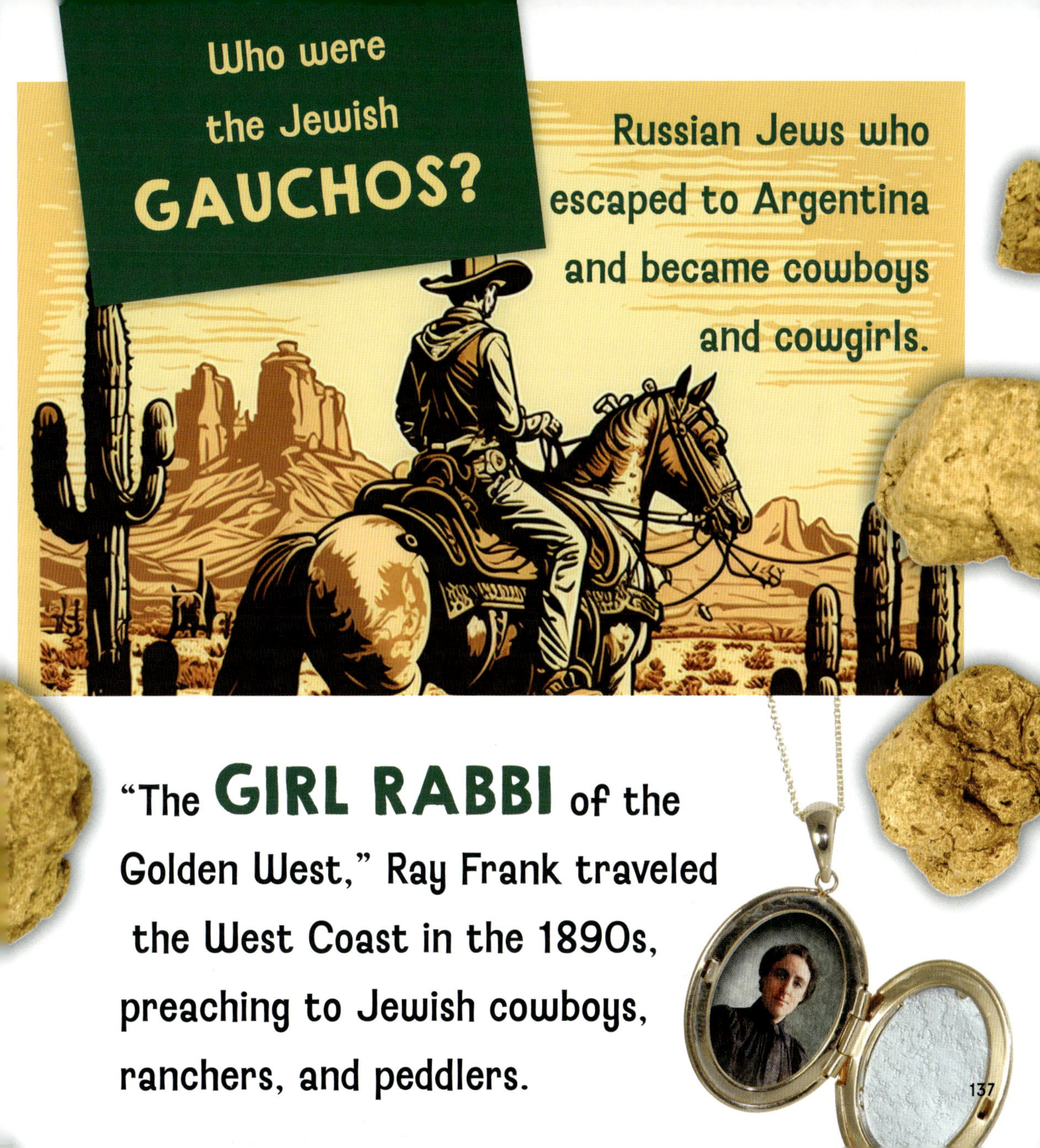

Who were the Jewish GAUCHOS?

Russian Jews who escaped to Argentina and became cowboys and cowgirls.

"The **GIRL RABBI** of the Golden West," Ray Frank traveled the West Coast in the 1890s, preaching to Jewish cowboys, ranchers, and peddlers.

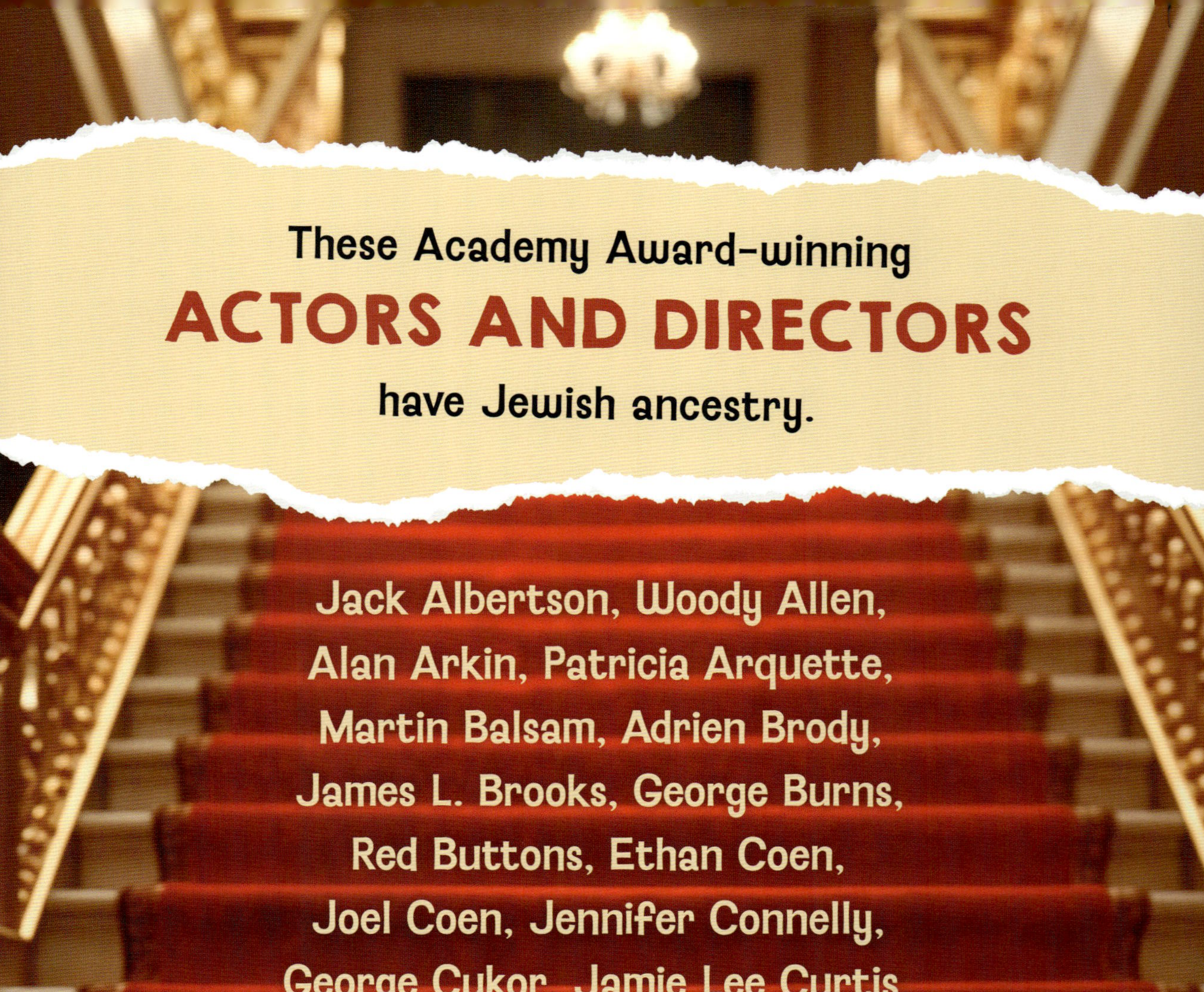

These Academy Award-winning

ACTORS AND DIRECTORS

have Jewish ancestry.

Jack Albertson, Woody Allen,
Alan Arkin, Patricia Arquette,
Martin Balsam, Adrien Brody,
James L. Brooks, George Burns,
Red Buttons, Ethan Coen,
Joel Coen, Jennifer Connelly,
George Cukor, Jamie Lee Curtis,
Michael Curtiz, Daniel Day-Lewis,
Melvyn Douglas, Michael Douglas,

Richard Dreyfuss, Miloš Forman,
William Friedkin, Lee Grant, Joel Grey,
Goldie Hawn, Michel Hazanavicius,
Dustin Hoffman, Judy Holliday, John Houseman,
Helen Hunt, Kevin Kline, Martin Landau,
Barry Levinson, Paul Lukas,
Joseph L. Mankiewicz, Marlee Matlin,
Walter Matthau, Sam Mendes, Lewis Milestone,
Paul Newman, Tatum O'Neal, Gwyneth Paltrow,
Sean Penn, Joaquin Phoenix, Roman Polanski,
Sydney Pollack, Natalie Portman, Luise Rainer,
Jerome Robbins, Joseph Schildkraut, John Schlesinger,
Norma Shearer, Simone Signoret, Steven Spielberg,
Oliver Stone, Barbra Streisand, Norman Taurog,
Elizabeth Taylor, Peter Ustinov, Rachel Weisz, Billy Wilder,
Shelley Winters, William Wyler, Fred Zinnemann.

HUMMUS ICE CREAM, anyone?

Apples and honey? Or olive oil?

Although these are real flavors in Israel, chocolate and vanilla still reign as the favorites.

Israel ranks in

7TH PLACE

worldwide for ice cream consumption.

Instead of drinking wine, Indian Jews eat **GRAPE SHERBET** on Shabbat and holidays.

Baskin-Robbins, Häagen-Dazs, and Ben & Jerry's were all **FOUNDED** by Jewish entrepreneurs.

Chazak, chazak, v'nitchazeik.

"Be strong, hold fast,
and let us strengthen one another."

It is traditional to say this Hebrew phrase when finishing a book of Torah.

Want to find out more?

Scan the QR code for a list of links for each of these facts.

Everybody in this book is Jewish except King Charles and the United States presidents. And, of course, Mr. Potato Head.

About the authors

Kerry Olitzky has been a congregational rabbi, a member of a rabbinical school faculty/administration, and an educational foundation executive and has also led a nonprofit organization. He and his wife are blessed with two rabbi sons and seven grandchildren. He lives in New Jersey.

Random fact: On top of all of that, he has been able to write 100 books—many while riding the New Jersey Transit commuter train into New York City, where he worked for 40 years.

Deborah Bodin Cohen is the rabbi of Beth Chai in Bethesda, Maryland. She previously served congregations in North Carolina and New Jersey. She's written a growing collection of books for Jewish children, teens, and families. She and her husband have three children—all who like memorizing odd trivia.

Random fact: She's distantly related to Nobel Prize winner Albert Abraham Michelson, who is featured in this book.

Image Sources Continued from Page 2 —

86 (bkgd) Kurz & Allison, 89 (sign) Esther Bubley. Flickr: 56B zeevveez. Shutterstock: 59B NYCStock, 106C Unai Huizi Photography, 107R Kzenon. Jewish Women's Archive: 64. The National Library of Israel: 73, 122-123L (historical photos) Dan Hadani Collection, The Pritzker Family National Photography Collection. Seth Kaller: 87R. Eric Etheridge: 89B. Freedom Forum's Newseum Collection: 88T Ted Polumbaum. New York Public Library Digital Collection: 96-97 (bkgd) Yiddish Theater Collection. Harry S. Truman Library: 103T. Top End Sports LLC: 113T Steven Le.